Apocalypse and Beyond...

By Phil Gibson

ISBN 978-1-291-22691-1

Dedication

For my father,

all I could ever hope to be;

David William Sumner Gibson,

(1938-2011)

Table of Contents

Forward

Apocalypse and Beyond is a compilation of poems from my previous anthologies, Apocalyptic Visions and Beyond the Mask, fleshed out with a selection of previously unpublished works for a total of 81 poems. Rather than presenting them alphabetically they have been arranged chronologically, in the order they were written. In this way my first poem, Apocalyptic Vision, the one penned after that moment of epiphany on a busy street many years ago (see the Foreword to my 1st book, Apocalyptic Visions), is presented in its rightful position - at the head of the collection.

The poem, Apocalyptic Vision, has special significance for me as it was the first. It was written during the winter of 1990-91 as the world held its breath awaiting the inevitability of the 1st Gulf War. At the time I was living in the attic of an isolated tumble-down bungalow on the Lizard Peninsula in Cornwall, struggling to survive on little money and less hope for the future as I mourned a love lost. By night I drank and wandered the rugged Lizard Downs, often finding myself at the cliff top above The Point, by day I slept off the night before. I felt my life could get no lower. Then everything changed...

On a crisp winter's day I aimlessly wandered the streets of Helston during a rare daytime visit to civilization, noticing the shoppers going about their day little more than they noticed me. I was pulled up suddenly by a strange noise that was not so much heard over the bustle that surrounded me as felt under it; a kind of throbbing vibration in my breast and temple that droned on and on, louder and louder. I looked about in confusion to find the source and saw that no-one else was reacting, the crowd simply parted about me with a mutter and a scowl at my obstruction of their vital journey. Slowly my gaze was drawn upwards as I realised the noise came from above, beyond the low hanging blanket of cloud, as comprehension washed over me like cold rain. I was hearing aero-engines, big ones. Some-where high above this small town English street large aircraft droned across the sky, bringing to mind US B-52 heavy bombers en-route to the Persian Gulf. The throbbing reverberation rumbled on, increasing to a dull roar that surely even the most ardent bargain hunter could not ignore, and yet they did, paying more attention to the obvious lunatic staring dumbly at the sky and blocking their path to the sale signs.

At that precise moment I had an epiphany. I immediately purchased a pen and note-book and boarded the first bus home, sketching out the bare bones of the first couple stanzas of my Apocalyptic Vision by the time I reached the bungalow. I retreated to the attic, my garret, and continued to write...

Everything in this collection is a direct expression of that moment...

A Glimpse Beyond the Horror of Phil Gibson

UK poet Phil Gibson can make you squirm and fear the dark while you are standing in broad daylight.

A Poe for the 21st century, Gibson's tell-tale heart is mankind's destruction of the planet that we call home. The horror of Phil's poetry is amplified by the brutal honesty of the crimes we commit against the environment and each other.

From the opening lines of *A Glimmer of Light* through to the closing lines of the Alice Cooper induced nightmares of *The Treatment* Phil Gibson's poems will have you reaching for the bedside lamp tonight...not just for light but as a weapon to ward off the demons that are sure to invade your thoughts and dreams.

If it is a nightmare that you are looking for this Halloween or an excuse to alarm others put down *The Raven* and pick up Phil Gibson's book.

Phil's *Prosperity Calls* from *Apocalyptic Visions* exemplifies his concerns for the environment and was featured on The Bar None Group website in the summer of 2011.

Bar None Publishing Group, OCTOBER 25, 2011

Apocalyptic Vision

Our world was dying, slow but sure
Whole species gone forever more
The rivers ran with filth and slime
The heavens stained with soot and grime
The poisoned sea, the barren land
And all this caused by human hand
In man's remorseless quest for power
He pillaged nature's sacred bower
Without a thought where it may lead
His one desire to sate his greed

But still mankind was not content
On self-destruction he seemed bent
As noxious vapours heat the sky
The crops all fail, the cattle die
The deserts grow, the graves do fill
The famines spread and yet man still
Let populations grow unchecked
While bones of folly vultures pecked
As man careered madly on
Not happy 'til his world was gone

Then trouble in the east began
All started by one Arab man
Who saw his neighbours land and wealth
And planned to take them for himself
He sent his troops in without warning
Resistance crushed in just one morning
The nations of the world enraged
In futile talks of peace engaged
To find solutions just and fair
While armies of the world prepare

And so the mighty warlords met
They talked of peace, they smiled and yet
They left that room with war in mind
A reason for it yet to find
Until a fireball in the east
Provoked the slumbering Hebrew beast
Long suffering they could take no more
They gave that Arab his holy war
Star of David burning bright
Set the Arab world alight

The time had come, the war begun
The battle that could not be won
The bells of doom began to toll
As war machines began to roll
And devils laughed and danced with mirth
Hell's fury loosed upon the Earth
As mighty metal beasts that crawl
And spit out fire and death for all
Began their slow futile advance
Began the Reaper's favourite dance

The fires of Hell were put to shame
As the world we knew was set aflame
And as the flames grew ever higher
For the human race, a funeral pyre
Black smoke obscured the noon daylight
The world engulfed in eternal night
By the war foretold by ancient seers
Ignored by man for a thousand years
Too late man sees the truth at last
The Apocalypse has come to pass

Poison and plague rain from the sky
A million men painfully die
Diseases spread throughout the land
Purposely placed by terror's hand
And in response, red buttons pressed
While keys are turned, excuses stressed
Resulting in man's greatest hour
Supreme expression of his power
To end his world by his own hand
In brief memorial mushrooms stand

The fighting stopped, a silence fell
Black rain quenched the fires of hell
The few survivors looked around
And saw the burned and blackened ground
The land was just a wasteland bare
No man or beast was moving there
But peace had come, the war was done
Though neither side had really won
In fact the human race had lost
And few were left to count the cost

But peoples of the world be calm
Your leaders they are safe from harm
Beneath the ground they lie in wait
Like beasts of prey, consumed with hate
And when the land again is green
They will emerge, a sight obscene
To start the human race anew
To take control, the chosen few
They'll lead us as they did before
Along the beaten path to War

Parasite

Imagine, if you will, our world
As some great beast, in sleep it's curled
Its blood, the rivers deep and long
Its bones, the mountains, proud and strong
Its organs, oceans and the seas
Its lungs, the forests, life they breathe

But as the beast in sleep does lie
It knows not it is doomed to die
For as it slumbers through the years
A tiny parasite appears
It quickly spreads across the beast
And on its life begins to feast

This infestation without sense
Unchecked it grows in virulence
And as the beast sleeps all the while
Pollutes its blood with poisons vile
That flow through hardened arteries
Into the organs of the seas

And still this pestilence was rife
It cut into the lungs of life
But as it ate into the bones
Leeching the minerals from the stones
The beast began to feel the pain
Too late it tried to stir again

With horror then the beast saw all
The carnage caused by pests so small
Like insects on its back they crawled
Like mighty nests their cities sprawled
Like worms they burrowed in its skin
It knew not where it could begin

Within the beast an anger burned
As fiery emotions churned
Erupting as a searing flood
That shook its bones and boiled its blood
The cities burned, the mountains fell
The beast unleashed the gates of hell

But when the smoke of fires cleared
The parasites again appeared
From holes where they had gone to hide
Their heads kept down, the storm to ride
And when the beast did see them there
Its anger died, it knew despair

And so the beast was filled with woe
It mourned itself, its tears did flow
And as it wept the waters rose
Inexorably drowning those
Who'd come to cause it so much pain
Now soon it would be cleansed again

The beast it saw and ceased to weep
Then settled right back down to sleep
Content the parasite was gone
It failed to notice there upon
A mountain stood a group of men
Who planned to start it all again

Genesis

There was a time when we weren't here
But then God had a good idea
He took a shapeless lump of clay
And formed this earth in just one day
And when He said, "Let there be light!"
Up popped the sun, all clear and bright
And cast its gold illumination
On God's sparkling new creation

Then He made the waters flow
And caused the trees and grass to grow
He brought forth fish to swim the seas
And fowl to nest within the trees
And called forth beasts to roam the land
All formed from clay by His own hand

But on the sixth and final day
One creative thought did go astray
And where it fell upon the ground
Man sprang up and looked around
He saw this land straight from God's heart
And began to take it all apart

Prophet's Lament

In this world of power gone mad
Alone I sit, forlorn and sad
I see the way that things will go
But wonder if to let man know
The time left to us is so brief
This so called gift brings so much grief

Future events before me lie
I see them all but wonder why
This weighty task was laid on me
Oh how I wish I could be free

Inside I know what I should do
But don't know if I'll bother to
Does mankind deserve to be saved
After the way that he's behaved?
This earth so pure when man first breathed
But now about it death is wreathed

I know that I should make a stand
That I should try to save this land
But will the people heed my cry
Or ridicule me as they die?

Brainstorm

My brain goes into overdrive
Unwanted thoughts unwilled arrive
Cascading in an endless flood
That clouds my mind like churned up mud

Ideas briefly tantalize
I grab for them but realize
It's pointless as they fade again
Into the mire from whence they came

Prisoner

Prisoner, longing to break free
Drowning in mediocrity
Confined by mundane existence
Condemned at birth, a life sentence

Restricted by reality
Manacled by mortality
My soul cries out and craves release
Maybe in death it will find peace

Visions

I saw the tables, round and white
All lit by dim and distant light
About them suited yuppies crowd
They're talking all at once so loud
Each one to their own mobile phone
Each one in his own world alone

And now, in groups of three or four
They stand with heads upon the floor
White tabletops upon their backs
Incessant talking never slacks
They have to finalize the deal
To them, what happens is not real

And now their trousers take to flight
Their socks held up by garters tight
The tabletops still on their backs
The tablecloths are Union Jacks
But they are not round anymore
They're coffin shaped unlike before

They're on a vast turntable, turning
While in a pile their suits are burning
And all the while above them flew
On wings of bright red white and blue
Like vultures circling the dead
Huge sugar lumps, in pairs they're wed

The sugar lumps begin to fall
Like bombs exploding one and all
The yuppies all keep talking on
As if nothing at all were wrong
But as the last sugar lump drops
Eventually, the talking stops...

Rabbits!

Rabbits, rabbits every-where
Giant ones with stark white hair
They turn up here they pop up there
Those rabbits they just do not care
That they drive my mind to despair
And make me pull out all my hair
What they are doing isn't fair
They make me see them every-where
I find them lurking on the stair
Even at night my bed they share
Within my dreams they're always there
Parading with that bunny flair
Their pure white coats a dazzling glare
They even take me to their lair
They've made inside a golden pear
And show me all their silver-ware
I see them sitting in my chair
I look again and see a pair
I drink my tea, there's one in there
It grins as though its cheeks will tear
Its eyes fixed in a manic stare
That makes me feel I should beware
In case those bunnies, they should dare
To float right up into the air
And send my mind spinning else-where!

The Jumper

I have out-lived my usefulness
Rejected to my loneliness
Discarded here upon the shelf
My only company, myself

It is a dreadful truth to see
To know that no-body wants me
Of this sad fact there is no doubt
Who'd want me now, I'm too worn out

Before me now my life is played
As I sit here with edges frayed
Each fibre of my being stretched
My misery in creases etched

Unraveling, I wonder why
It came to this, I start to cry
I long for peace in endless sleep
With eyes closed, off the cliff I leap

A Rebel Dies

He lies upon the field alone
No-one to hear his dying moan
Nor hold his hand there as he dies
Or wipe the tears from his eyes

He knows his guts shot full of lead
And very soon now he'll be dead
The pain so great he can but weep
But soon in painless death he'll sleep

But as he lies there on the ground
He thinks not of the dead all round
Nor of his comrades left alive
Or if to find him they'll arrive

His thoughts ignore the Southern cause
Nor for a moment do they pause
Upon the unjust invasion
By northern troops of his nation

But one thing fills his reverie
A single face he'll no-more see
Of one he's loathe to leave behind
His dear wife's sweet smile fills his mind

Just at the moment that he dies
As fresh tears well up in his eyes
His last breath leaves his broken frame
It utters once more his wife's name

Now as he lies there still and cold
The misery seen left untold
His face set in a peaceful smile
Was all this suffering worthwhile?

The Weeping Soldier

The battle was over, the killing was done
The bodies lay bloating beneath the hot sun
I saw as I walked through the dead and the dying
A young rebel soldier, like a babe he was crying

Slumped on the ground in his torn dirty rags
His worldly possessions in two battered bags
No food in his belly, no boots of his own
He'd marched so for miles with never a moan

But now he sat weeping and broken at last
While stretched out before him upon the scorched grass
Lay a union soldier, but though he was dead
In his lap that young rebel still cradled his head

Then as I drew nearer his sad head he raised
And into my face his haunted eyes gazed
With fresh tears smudging the grime on his cheek
He choked back the sobs and then started to speak

"Please can you tell me, what are we fighting for?
When it started I knew but I don't anymore
Why can't we go back to our homes and our wives,
Put an end to this madness and get on with our lives?"

At first I was lost, didn't know what to say
I admit my first instinct was to walk away
But I wanted to comfort this grief-stricken man
So choosing my words this reply I began

"The yanks are our foe, they invaded our land
They want to subject us to their iron hand
We're fighting for honour and our liberty
Defending our homes from the north's treachery"

For a moment the soldier sat silently there
With one trembling hand gently stroking the hair
Of the head in his lap, as if he hadn't died
Then without looking up he slowly replied

"Though you see a Yankee just like any other
This man was no northerner, he was my brother
How could he invade a land that's his own?
Why ever did he turn his back on his home?

The last time I saw him was three years ago
When he said he was going I hated him so
For leaving his home for a union way
When he said farewell I had nothing to say

But now he is gone, slain by this bloody war
It's too late for talking, he'll hear me no more
I just wish I'd had time to tell him one thing
That whatever he did, I always loved him"

Listen, Do You Hear Them?

Listen, do you hear them?
In the quiet of the night
A million souls are crying
As they mourn the fading light
The darkness overwhelms them
As they huddle round the fire
Though they know the Sun is dying
They refuse to light the pyre

Dogmatic arches tumble round them
As they cling to every stone
Though the Advocate is lying
They still hear his words alone
But the shadows whisper to them
From dark reaches of the mind
And the Prophets sadly sighing
To the end he is resigned

Listen, do you hear them?
From dark caverns 'neath the ground
While above the corpses lying
There's no-one to hear the sound
No, there's no-body to hear them
All their pleas fall on dead ears
But they have to keep on trying
Through the swiftly darkening years

The Treatment

Alone I sit within my room
So small and painted white
Walls padded like my mother's womb
And lit by blinding light

Some-one behind, I don't know whom
Then draws my jacket tight
Into my view strange faces loom
And tell me it's alright

A needle's jab brings torpid doom
It does not help to fight
They lock me in my sterile tomb
You think this soothes my plight?

Hell on Earth

If there is a Prince of Darkness
And He is alive and well
I'm sure He would be more at home
On earth than down in Hell

Just take a look around you
And I'm sure you will agree
When you open up your eyes
To all the pain and misery

So when the churches try to scare you
With damnation, do not fear
I'm sure Hell must be empty
As the devils are all here

Who Am I?

Who am I?
Where am I?
What is this place?

Who are you?
What have you
Got on your face?

Is it mud?
Is it blood?
Oh what a waste

Why do we fight
Oh yes, that's right
We are the human race

Renewal

What is this pain within my head?
Am I alive or am I dead?
Why am I lost in endless night?
What is that blinding golden light?

Who is that distant silhouette?
Recalled from memories I forget
And why do echoes beckon me
To walk into that light I see?

But why am I now falling?
Whose voice do I hear calling?
It's dragging me, I'm sinking
I feel as though I'm shrinking

What is that rhythmic thumping?
What is this fluid pumping?
Why am I filled with so much dread?
What is that pressure on my head?

It pulls me from my waking dream
I open up my eyes and scream...

Waking Nightmare

I feel my mind is slowly lifting
Through hidden doors dark shades are drifting
Last ghosts of quickly fading dreams
Retreating forms of silent screams

In momentary silence lying
With unseen nightmare spectres dying
My drowsy sleep-thick mind is idling
Why is the air so warm and stifling?

I open up my eyes to see
But all is black, how can this be?
How can there be no shred of light?
My god, could I have lost my sight?

Why do I feel so stiff and sore?
Why am I lying on the floor?
So hard to move my arms from rest
Why are they folded on my chest?

I raise my hand to test eyes flawed
My knuckles graze against rough board
My elbows knock restricting sides
With horror then I realise

Like half-remembered memories
Nightmarish echoes surge with ease
From dark recesses of my brain
Where they were locked to save me pain

I hear the grieving mourners moaning
The distant solemn voice is droning
Of how life can be so unjust
Ash to ash and dust to dust

But these spectres are from no dream
No-one can hear but still I scream
My heart is filled with icy dread
They've buried me,
BUT I`M NOT DEAD!!

How Do You Know..?

How do you know
What you're seeing is real?
Is that which you touch
The same as you feel?
How can you be sure
What I think I have seen?
What you see as red
I may see as green.

The harder you think
The stranger it seems
Reality starts
To stretch at the seems

It's easy to fool
Your ears with a sound
Though words sound the same
Diverse meanings are found
Your eyes are as prone
To illusion, you'll find
Could it be as simple
To flummox the mind?

But how do we learn
To recognize truth?
We're programmed from birth
Indoctrined through youth
We see what we're told
We're told what to see
Schooled in the image
Of conformity

But now when you think of it
How do we know?
Just because parents
And teachers said so?
What makes them the experts
On reality?
They've no more idea
Than you have or me

So who makes the rules
We so blindly obey?
And who says the darkness
Of light follows day?

How do you know
I can't walk through a wall?
How can you tell
We exist here at all?
The whole of this life
Could just be a dream
Maybe in a moment
I'll wake with a scream

But what if this theory
Turned out to be true
Who would be the dreamer
Me, God, Satan or you?
Could this world all be
Your imagination?
Or maybe you're part
Of my dream creation?

But there is one truth
In life, it is said
That when it all ends
We all end up dead
Yet maybe it isn't
So clean cut and dried
Who knows what will happen
To us when we've died?

Though no-one can answer
These questions profound
They're certain to turn
Your brain upside down

So maybe these words
Have all been for naught
But I'd like to leave you
With one passing thought
Are you certain these words
Have always been here?
As you turn the next page
Maybe they'll disappear....?

Who's Mad?

They say I'm mentally deranged
For my own good they keep me caged
Within this room all padded white
Confined by jackets straps so tight
Locked in this cell with windows barred
They tell me that my brain is scarred

They treat me like a naughty child
Their condescending voices mild
With soothing words they humour me
Each time I try to make them see
That I am just as sane as they
But no-one hears a word I say

Why can't they see that they are wrong
In this place I do not belong
Although I know I am sane now
This place affects the brain somehow
At times I fear I'll lose my mind
If some way out I do not find

They tell me that I am insane
I'll never be set free again
For I've committed dreadful crimes
The foulest murders many times
But they just do not realize
That I know all their words are lies

Men in white coats are always there
But I know they don't really care
They say they wish to ease my pain
But keep me drugged to dull my brain
Preventing me from thinking straight
It's them who fill my mind with hate

This place is filled with maniacs
At night I hear their rage attacks
They infiltrate sedated dreams
Torment me with demented screams
That's why my memory is filled
With images of those they've killed

This place is taking hold of me
The voices whisper constantly
I must ignore the things they say
But they grow stronger every day
I'm lost unless I break this cage
For now the voices scream with rage!

Savage in a Suit

You think you are so civilized
But it is time you realized
How easily cracks can appear
In your so finely groomed veneer

We're just a couple of meals away
From anarchy, so experts say
I'm sure you doubt this can be true
So I'll try to enlighten you

The basic instinct in us all
Before which all the others fall
Is that to keep yourself alive
At all costs you have to survive

Imagine now some future date
When all the world's long pent-up hate
Erupts into the final war
The Establishment exists no more

The things you take for granted now
They are no longer there somehow
No petrol for your fancy car
Well, am I getting through so far?

No food will reach your local store
Your power and water flow no more
Gangs and looters roam the night
Now there is no electric light

But things will go from bad to worse
With worthless money in your purse
No matter, there's no food to buy
And anyway, the end is nigh

Soon shortages will start to bite
Out on the streets the people fight
For any food that does arrive
Remember, they have to survive

At first the law enforcers try
But soon they start to wonder why
They bother with a fruitless quest
They're in the same boat as the rest

And that is when the end will start
When our society falls apart
No-one to keep the mob in check
The rats have left the sinking wreck

They talk of concrete jungles now
But they just don't compare somehow
To millions of our charming race
Competing in a real rat race

Countless starving millions dying
On the streets the corpses lying
And those unlucky ones alive
With only one thought, to survive

Could you survive this brave new world
When anarchy's flag is unfurled?
Or would you just curl up and die
Cowering as your children cry?

Something Missing

Adrift in an ocean
Of shattered illusions
Broken spirits battered
By karmic contusions
Desperately seeking
For that which is lost
Trying to capture
A forgotten ghost

Unknowingly craving
A meaning to life
But dull apathetic
Inertia is rife
Both feet firmly planted
In life sapping earth
To wonders of being
We're blinded at birth

Overwhelmed by a sense
Of loss that is burning
For something unknown
Our souls cry out, yearning
Announcing with flippance
Our proud disbelief
But secretly harbouring
Unexplainable grief

Lost in a culture
Motivated by greed
We don't understand
Just what we really need
But we keep on searching
Though havoc we spread
Maybe we'll never find it
Until we are dead

Testing, testing...

Could we all be on
Some great cosmic quest?
Could this life all be
Some kind of a test
But what if we fail?
What would happen then?
Would we be sent back
To do it again?
But if that were true
How can you be sure
That what you do now
You've not done before?
But then that would mean
You're doing it wrong
And you'll be back here
Again before long...

Christmas Cheer

So soon that time is here again
Of peace and goodwill to all men
The passing of another year
Church bells ring out the Christmas Cheer

Green holly hanging on the doors
The streets are filled with Santa Claus
You'll find him there in every store
Surrounded by fine gifts galore

But this year will you spare a thought
For all the poor children with naught?
Or will you just repeat last year
And lose yourself in Christmas Cheer?

Lost

I'm wandering lost
In an alien land
Cast out in a world
I don't understand
Wistfully gazing
Through mist laden eyes
At vitriol clouds
In thermal glass skies

Pestilent deserts
Stretch mile upon mile
Pockmarked by copses
Of skeletons vile
Blackened and twisted
Limbs reach for the sky
A miasmal breeze
Passes through with a sigh

My eyes start to fill
As onward I roam
Past festering rivers
That bubble and foam
Foul gurgling cocktails
With flotsam of death
Like open-cast sewers
With venomous breath

To the horizon
My stinging eyes gaze
Vast tombstones are rising
Through death dealing haze
Cancerous tumours
Malignant they stand
Belching forth black fumes
To poison the land

I stumble half blind
Now sobbing with grief
My mind in a whirl
Of cruel disbelief
This vision of Hell
Seen blurred by my tears
Will be my own world
Or has been for years

Labyrinth

I'm standing at an intersection
Mind in a whirl, I'm so confused
Bewildered by choice of direction
I wonder how many have mused
At this point with no way to know
Which is the safest way to go

Before me now the choices stand
Dark corridors to different lives
But there's no way to understand
Where any one of them arrives
Voices urge me to plunge headlong
Into black holes that may be wrong

I can't decide, I hesitate
Pressure builds 'til I want to scream
Yet if I wait it'll be too late
I wish this could all be a dream
But is this life or is it Hell?
There is no way for me to tell

I had a map, a plan to follow
But it was torn out of my heart
It left me wandering in sorrow
So lost with no clue where to start
But now I'm overwhelmed with voices
Hounding me with their own choices

I must keeping moving, I can't stay here
Through time the beast is stalking me
I hear his icy breath draw near
It's adding to my misery
It means I have to choose a door
And leave my past for Ever Moor

Ever Moor

I'm on the path to Ever Moor
A place I've never seen before
But it's a place I'll never find
It's lost in mists within my mind

Some roads lead left, some paths lead right
Some brightly lit, some cloaked in night
Whatever different signs may say
You'll find they all still lead one way

No matter how you make your plan
No matter from whence you began
Where-ever you are heading for
All paths still lead to Ever Moor

A Revelation

I dreamt I saw the sea on fire
But as the flames began to fade
I saw the self-proclaimed Messiah
He rode a jackass motorcade
Wearing his crown of razor wire
Through green stained blood I saw him wade

A silhouette in the setting sun
Twelve star disciples in his hand
He said His great work had begun
His golden creed spread through the land
The time had come, His will be done
I'd either die or understand

To my mind came a revelation
The present's future past to come
All people of the world, one nation
A view of paradise to some
United in annihilation
All creeds together, every one

Hopeless Glory

The flag is raised, the cry goes out
"IT'S WAR!" the tabloid headlines shout
The country rallies to the cause
Aggression rips the peaceful gauze

We fight for peace and human rights
We're off to set the world to rights
A chance to revel in the glory
A sequel to the same old story

We see the boys off with loud cheers
Their loved ones shed a few proud tears
But it's a time to celebrate
They're off to crush the ones we hate

But as the troops sail from our shore
We somehow lose touch with the war
Our gallant boys, of course we care
But all the fighting's over there

The gung-ho spirit stays alive
Until the body bags arrive
And when the casualty lists grow
Most people just don't want to know

The wounded, blinded, scarred and maimed
Burnt by our fervour's fire inflamed
The shell-shocked, weary and insane
And countless free from further pain

They've paid the price for you and me
To keep our country's liberty
But now they've no more part to play
Ungratefully we walk away

Running Scared

Hiding out
I'm on the run
Keeping low
I trust no-one
Dodging, evading
Drab columns parading
Rumbling convoys
All roads are filled
Crushing the corpses
Of those they've killed

I flee to the trees
Disappearing with ease
But there I behold
A terrible truth
Littering leaf mold
The flower of youth
Each wearing a bracelet
Of glistening scarlet
Each branch and each limb
Dripping bright scarlet trim

But now I am trapped
In a tumble down shack
A wasted corpse rises
The final attack
It lunges at me
Knife clutched in its hand
But carves for itself
A scarlet wristband

I wake with a scream
I'm dripping with sweat
It was only a dream
Unreal and yet
What could it all mean?
What was it all for?
Could these things I've seen
Be foretelling war?

Pressure Valve

These words are my emotional valve
Soothing wounds that have no salve
Releasing pressure from head and heart
That threatens to tear my soul apart

Though they do not remove the pain
In some small way they ease the strain
Of feelings long pent-up within
Behind a barrier so thin

So if these words mean nothing to you
Maybe you're one of those lucky few
Who take all life's knocks in their stride
With no emotional scars to hide

Curtain Call

The show is coming to an end now
It's time to turn down all the lights
There will be no more sunny days now
There will only be dark endless nights

The curtains will be coming down now
To the silent sound of tears
The orchestra has long been dead now
The audience died through the years

There will be no more cries for encore
And no bouquets thrown on the stage
Because the cast is not there anymore
To see the dawning Golden Age

Despite the Author's best intentions
And of the Director, His Son
The leading man made new inventions
For gain he slaughtered everyone

So all the lights are going dim now
All fading quickly one by one
The Author starts to write again now
Another story has begun

Littered Streets

In every city, every town
Discarded, lying on the ground
An unacknowledged legacy
Of our throwaway society

When out of sight it's out of mind
But you're as likely now to find
This problem in a shop doorway
As hidden in an alleyway

We all walk past it everyday
But turn our eyes the other way
There's no solution we can see
It's not our responsibility

But if it's not for us to solve
Then whose job is it to resolve
This tragedy of modern life
This deprivation now so rife

So when you next walk down the street
So smart with new shoes on your feet
Just pause and ponder, do you care
About the homeless huddled there?

Terminal Case

Now this really is a most interesting case
But I'm sorry to say we're losing the race
To halt the infection, it's spreading too fast
The way things are going the subject won't last

We're dealing here with a most virulent strain
As you see the life signs are all on the wane
This must be the worst case that we've ever seen
That's why we are keeping it in quarantine

The parasite is quite a devious one
By disguising itself as a symbion
It managed to spread undetected with ease
It just wasn't recognized as a disease

But when it was ready it raised its vile head
From then on the subject was as good as dead
The parasite then launched a ruthless assault
On all natural functions almost without fault

But it multiplies with such alarming speed
Devouring its host with insatiable greed
I'm sorry to say there's no cure we can find
This world has a terminal case of mankind

How long?

How long will our eyes
Remain blind to the pain?
When will we realize
That our hands bear the stain
From the blood of the lives
Thrown away for our gain?

How long will our ears
Remain deaf to the cries
Of the orphan who fears
As his family dies?
How long 'til some-one hears
Truth behind all the lies?

How long before we
Sense the smell in the air
Of death and misery
Now so rife everywhere?
How long will it be
Before we show we care?

How long before we
Taste the salt of the tears
That have flown to the sea
In the shadows for years?
How long will it be
Until new light appears?

How long will our hearts
Remain numb to the pain?
When new suffering starts
Will we ignore it again
Or follow our hearts
And end misery's reign?

Tomorrow's Legacy

How will you explain to grandchildren to come
Why they cannot go out and play in the sun
Without some kind of ultra-violet screen
How will you explain the plain truth so obscene?

How will you explain why they can't go outside
Without an air filter behind which to hide?
Or maybe it won't be so hard to because
They'll never have known what fresh air really was

How will you explain that it's your legacy
That stops them from taking a dip in the sea?
And will you explain that there once was a time
When all the world's oceans were not lifeless slime?

How will you explain the lost beauty of trees?
How will you describe rustling leaves in the breeze?
When you tell them about living carpets of green
Will they comprehend something they've never seen?

How will you explain to a future grandchild
That animals used to run free in the wild
When he's only seen a selection so few
Who live wretched lives locked away in the zoo?

How will you explain how the world used to be
Before it succumbed to man's insanity?
How will you explain why you stood idly by
And let your grandchildren's inheritance die?

God Save the Children

God save the children
From the troubles of this life
Shield them and protect them
From the heartache and the strife

God save the children
Dry their tears when they cry
When the world mistreats them
Do not turn a blinded eye

God save the children
Cold and lonely in life's rain
Shelter them and feed them
They just don't deserve the pain

God save the children
Do not listen to the lie
Of those who'd exploit them
Do not let the children die

God save the children
All our hopes they will fulfill
Some-one has to save them
As no-body down here will!

A Painful Truth

A figure of death
Looms over the land
A nuclear scythe
Is borne in his hand
Wearing a mantle
Of consuming fire
He lights for our world
A funeral pyre

I flee in terror
But find no escape
For all of this land
Shows signs of his rape
Where-ever I go
He is always there
Stripping the land
And leaving it bare

I hear his cruel laughter
A malicious sound
While his victims' corpses
Are thick on the ground
He's dealing out death
And pain on a whim
There can be no way
Of hiding from him

But now I am running
So desperate to hide
For I've glimpsed a truth
I cannot abide
The horror flows through me
For now I can see
There is no escape
This figure is me!

Shadows in the Light

I see a shadow in a cloak of darkness
Lurking at the edge of the circle of light
I see a finger of pale bone beckon
Urging me to walk into the night

I hear the rustle of unearthly whispers
Echoes of the souls who have gone before
I hear the distant sound of ghostly laughter
Tempting me to seek the truth and more

I smell the scent of death is all around me
Gagging me as I leave the light for the gloom
I smell the fetid stench of rotting corpses
Wafting from the desecrated tomb

I taste the sourness of my bile rising
Stumbling as I see that no-one understands
I taste the bitter blood of murdered innocence
Dripping scarlet from my own two hands

I feel the icy clutch of terror grip me
Weighing down my limbs and drawing out my breath
I feel my empty body falling lifeless
Another voice in the chorus of death

Morbidity

I have a dream, a fantasy
Where all men live in harmony
An end to pain and enmity
A new birth for humanity

Each day I wake reluctantly
And come back to reality
I look around in misery
And see the true insanity

A world ruled by brutality
Supported by complacency
We're in the grip of tyranny
Choked by our own misanthropy

The masses in obscurity
Condemned to live in poverty
A life of harsh severity
The cruelest immorality

Each day a new atrocity
Will reach new depths of cruelty
We're sinking into savagery
A slow death for humanity

New Life, Old Death

As each new day breaks round the world
A precious plaintive cry is heard
A new life drawing its first breath
Beginning on the road to death

This miracle of life's new birth
Another victim for this earth
And man's depravity run wild
What kind of life for this new child?

For each child born another dies
Murdered by this world of lies
And no-one sees the mother's tears
Or understands her pain of years

So many wasted innocents
Consumed by man's malevolence
But do not fill your heart with scorn
Rejoice; another child is born!

Waiting

I'm just killing time
While time is killing me
Remembering a time
That is yet to be
I'm just standing still
Going no-where fast
Waiting for a moment
Coming out of my past

I'm strolling on the brink
Of my sanity
Carrying the burden
Of humanity
I'm watching life bloom
Then wither away
Moments glitter briefly
But they never stay

I'm counting each grain
Of sand that is falling
Hearing all the ghosts
Of past lives calling
I'm feeling each grain
Bring me nearer the door
Waiting for the time
To shed this skin once more

Circular Road

The road of life is long and hard
You step upon it from the womb
Each breath you take another yard
That brings you nearer to the tomb

The way is strewn with obstacles
It seems you'll never reach the end
And you can never see pit-falls
Hiding round the coming bend

At times you just can take no more
And wonder what would happen if
You took the scarlet signed detour
The path that leads you to the cliff

But in time all your bruises mend
And all the sharp short cuts apart
You make it to the bitter end
And find yourself back at the start

Lamented Youth

I want to live but long to die
I laugh aloud, inside I cry
I'm crowded in my loneliness
My brain is filled with emptiness

But am I mad or just insane?
My mood swings black and blue again
My mind is in a dreadful spin
My grip on life is oh so thin

But all around me life goes on
As if nothing at all was wrong
Why is it no-one else can see
Just what is happening to me?

I'm raging at the world in pain
My cries for help are all in vain
No-body hears my silent scream
They live their life in their own dream

Shadow Secrets

Standing at the window
I stare into the night
I wonder what is out there
Hiding from the light

Shadows growing deeper
An impenetrable wall
Throwing off the moonlight
Hiding secrets from us all

Rustles from the darkness
Tell of horrors yet unseen
But when I look they vanish
Just as if they've never been

Shadows seem to whisper
Telling tales of the vain
Who dared to seek the answers
And were never seen again

But I know they are out there
Shadows lurking in the night
Denizens of darkness
Hiding from the light

Another Lonely Day

As the sun is sinking
On another lonely day
I just cannot help thinking
How can I go on this way?

Days and nights are merging
Into one long drawn out pain
Memories converging
Into one more tear in vain

All alone I'm lying
As the days just pass me by
All my dreams are dying
How long can I live this lie?

Now the day is sleeping
As the night is drawing in
All alone I'm weeping
Soon a new day will begin

The Fall

Just the ticking of the seconds
Dragging out another year
As the coffin faintly beckons
Just another dripping tear
Falling wetly from my eyes
To the scarred and blackened ground
As another victim dies
No solution can be found

Just the beating of the heart
Keeping rhythm, timing death
As the world is torn apart
Take another dying breath
Of the poison laden air
Draw it deep into your soul
Do not worry, they don`t care
Without corruption you`re not whole

Just another passing fashion
New life in an older form
As an all consuming passion
Takes the world by silent storm
Spreading hope for new beginning
But the truth is far from true
As the noxious air is thinning
They still take their cash from you

Just another wasted tear
Falling where the corpses lie
Why can no-body else hear
All the dead and dying cry
Crying out for our salvation
And an end to all their pain
They see our looming damnation
But they`re just ignored again

Poppy Petals

Lonely dripping scarlet tears
Spread their stain across the years
Silent rivulets of blood
Go unnoticed in the mud

Blood stained crosses stand in rows
As the single bugle blows
Poppy petals in the breeze
Hide the unseen agonies

By the rusty barbed wire fence
Water fills the empty trench
Where so much young blood was spilt
And yet the guilty feel no guilt

Prosperity Calls

The charges are set
We're ready to blast
There's no need to worry
The mountain will last
This rubble is needed
For factory walls
We've no time to rest
Prosperity calls

Stoke up the furnace
Don't let the fire die
Keep the coal coming
An endless supply
We must keep producing
There's more fuel to burn
The darkness at noon
Is not our concern

There's no time to rest
There're more trees to fell
The more we cut down
The more we can sell
It's all they are good for
They're dead anyway
Soaked in pollution
To wither away

Send out the trawlers
With wall of death nets
There must be an hour
Before the sun sets
We have to work harder
The only solution
There's less fish to catch
That's man's contribution

The pressure is mounting
Our profits are down
There's no time for sleeping
Get up off the ground
There's so little time left
We have to get on
Why is it so dark?
Where has our world gone?

Inspiration

A soaring of the spirit
As the inner mind expands
A power surge of insight
Flowing white hot to the hands

Exhilaration burning
As pure reason is surpassed
But now the truth eludes me
One more fleeting moment passed

No Compost Mennis

There are toys in my attic
But the marbles have gone
There is no-body up there
But the light is still on

Though the lift is still working
It won't go to the top
A screw has worked itself loose
And it made the lift stop

There are bats in my belfry
And their chatter has no end
So I climbed off my rocker
Up the pole and round the bend

Now I'm free, I'm out to lunch
All the fairies are there
We're dining with the Hatter
And the rabid March Hare

The Candle

The candle flame is burning bright
A humble source of simple light
And yet this candle wakes in me
A view of our mortality

As I watch the candle burn away
Just as our world burns day by day
Its soot and smoke pollute the air
No-one around me seems to care

Dark shadows dance upon the wall
Like devils come to watch our fall
They gather round the dying flame
And laugh as we apportion blame

And as I watch the flame burn low
With horrid certainty I know
Just like the candle fading fast
Our species reign on earth won't last

Rollercoaster

Ride the rollercoaster
As it thunders through your mind
You're strapped into the front seat
And the operators blind

Accelerating downwards
You cannot suppress a scream
There is no-one here to save you
This is really not a dream

You plunge into the dark depths
As your heart begins to sink
You stare into insanity
As you totter on the brink

Just when you can take no more
And you scream for it to stop
Your stomach takes a back seat
As you soar back to the top

You claw your way back upwards
'til you reach the dizzy heights
And rest there for a moment
In the heavens starry lights

Though this reprieve is only brief
For now you do not care
That very soon you'll plunge once more
Into some new nightmare

Nemesis

Looming shadows drawing near
Darkness borne on wings of fear
Foot-steps echo close behind
Conjured spectres plague your mind
Lurking in the endless night
Stalking you as you take flight
As your nerve breaks start to run
Race of Death has now begun
Icy breath, spine-chilling touch
Blood runs cold, cadaver's clutch
A tightened grip, you can't break loose
You're hanging in a rigid noose
Your chest is tight, your heart expands
You're clawing at those vice-like hands
You know your heart can't take the strain
You're blinded by its bursting pain
You feel your soul is fading fast
Your life's events are flashing past
There is no need to struggle now
You know this pain will end somehow
With open arms embrace Death's bliss
You can't escape your Nemesis

Puzzle of Tears

The pieces slot together
Like a puzzle in the rain
You can see the picture forming
But you have to hide your pain

You cannot reveal your fears
Of the things you dread the most
As another fragment settles
Raking up another ghost

Though today is looking sunny
In the future shadows lurk
You are trying to ignore them
But your bluffing doesn't work

You are looking to the future
As you hope your love will last
But you're haunted by the spectres
Looming at you from the past

<u>Emerald Flame</u>

A fire infernal
That rages internal
It burns through your brain
And drives you insane

Irrational fears
And unexplained tears
Emotions inflamed
The innocents blamed

Unfounded suspicions
Imagined deceptions
Your misery grows
But no-body knows

The Mirror

Mirror, mirror on the wall
Please tell me who I am
Show the things inside
And not the outer man
Reveal to me truth
Of that which lies within
And not the veil of lies
Wrapped up in mortal skin

I'm staring in the face
Of my insanity
There's something looking back
I'm sure it isn't me
It's staring back at me
Through dark foreboding eyes
Using my reflection
Its gossamer disguise

Malevolence burns deep
Within those orbs of pain
Accusing me of life
And driving me insane
Revulsion wells inside
As I destroy the glass
I wish I didn't know
What lurks behind that mask

Billboard Prophet

The billboard prophet prowls the city streets
He's preaching doom and gloom to all he meets
"Repent you sinners for the end is nigh!"
They hear the prophet's well known battle cry

He says The Judgement Day is drawing near
But no-one on the street has time to hear
To them their time is measured by its gain
And anyway, this old man is insane

But why does every-body hurry by?
Uneasy glances as they hear his cry
Maybe they don't think he is such a fool
Could he know something they should all know too?

But he is just an old and lonely man
He has no secret knowledge of life's plan
He is just a man with opened eyes
Who sees the truth as our world slowly dies

Morbid, Who Me?

There is a question
I have been asked
now so many times;
I'm always asked
why do I have to
write depressing rhymes?

These people say
that I should write
of pleasant happy things,
Describing pretty
flowers and
the way the songbird sings.

They ask me why
I cannot write
of love and peace and joy,
Portraying laughing
children playing
with a favourite toy.

They say that I
should tell of all
the beauty of this land,
I try to give
my answer but
they do not understand.

The reason is
so clear to me,
why can't they realize?
I cannot write
these things for then
I would be telling lies.

The sad fact is
this world is full
of hatred, war and pain,
A world in which
the children are
locked up and go insane.

They dug up all
the flowers, shot
the birds out of the sky,
I cannot write
of beauty as
I watch that beauty die.

Peace In Our Time (1992)

To see peace in a modern sense
Just look to Lebanon
In Beirut's battered city streets
The fighting still goes on

In what was Yugoslavia
They're fighting once again
The U.N. called a cease-fire
But their efforts are in vain

And close to home in Belfast
Where the Troubles still go on
Where soldiers armed with empty guns
Face the bullet and the bomb

Religion fights religion
And the Arab fights the Jew
And dogs of war fight every-one
If they are paid their due

And no-one seems contented
Unless settling a score
There's only one more thing to say
Thank god there is no war!

Shell-shocked

My head is throbbing dully
As I slowly come around
And at first I can't remember
Why I'm lying on the ground

But then it all comes back to me
As my mind is clear at last
A deafening explosion
As the ground shook with the blast

I try to look around me
As I peer through the haze
But have to shield my blistered face
A vehicle's ablaze

A twisted hunk of metal
By a hole there in the ground
Then the ringing in my ears stops
And I hear the dreadful sounds

A low and mournful moaning
Punctuated now by screams
The voice of utter terror
Never heard in my worst dreams

I look around in disbelief
At a vision straight from hell
All about me twisted bodies
Lying broken where they fell

The twitching human debris
Writhing, moaning with the pain
As the shocked and stunned survivors
Pick their way through the remains

But there is not one uniform
On the murdered and the slain
Not one of them were paid
To throw their lives away in vain

For this was once a crowded street
Where no-one knew or cared
'Til they became the victims
In a war no-one declared

The Voice

There's a voice on the phone
Telling me I'm not at home
So I'll hide and pretend that I'm not here

There's a voice at the door
And it knows I'm on the floor
So I curl up and try to disappear

There's a voice in the room
It can see me in the gloom
So I try to hide the scent of my fear

There's a voice in my brain
And it tells me I'm insane
Now the mist in my mind starts to clear

There's a voice in my head
And it's telling me I'm dead
Now the Reaperman in black has appeared

Love Is...

Love is a blessing
But also a curse
There's nothing else better
But nothing else worse
Love raises the spirits
Or drives you to drink
It makes you inspired
Or so you can't think
Love heals old wounds
But its scars never mend
It produces new life
And brings lives to an end
But whatever the pleasures
Whatever the pain
I know I could not live
Without love again

A Glimmer of Light

My eyes slip out of focus
As my sight is drawn within
Now my conscious mind is sinking
As the images begin

My thoughts like liquid lightning
Slip elusive through my mind
Kaleidoscopic visions
Leave me stumbling and blind

Embryonic inspirations
Glitter briefly out of sight
As my mind tries to embrace them
They just fade into the light

In a torment of frustration
At deficiencies of soul
Imperfections of pure reason
Leave me clutching for my goal

I have glimpsed a true illusion
That surpassed my simple thought
I have tried to scratch the surface
But my efforts came to naught

<u>Childish Tears</u>

I can see a child crying
As he hugs his injured knee
And a feeling of such sorrow
Is awakened there in me

I can see the child's tears
Falling softly to the ground
I can hear his tearful sobbing
And I'm haunted by the sound

For I know a time is coming
When the children all will cry
As they wonder why their parents
Let the world around them die

The Return of the Rabbit

You could ask the giant rabbit
With his dazzling white hair
You could ask the little piggies
Running home without a care
You could ask the talking walrus
Or the carpenter, his friend
You could ask the little oysters
As they run to meet their end
You could ask the flying toadstools
With their red and yellow spots
You could ask the laughing zebra
As he joins in all their dots
You could ask the giant cockroach
Sitting there upon my bed
You could ask the grinning ashtray
Sitting waiting to be fed
You could ask them all one question
And then ask them once again
And they'd all give you one answer
There's no way that I'm insane

The Wisdom of a Child

Children playing in the street
Laughing voices, running feet
Life for them is just a game
Innocent and free from blame

Far too soon will come the day
When these children move away
On the road to adulthood
Childish games are gone for good

Then those children, they will be
No different to you or me
They will blame their fellow man
For this mess we all began

If only we could view this earth
With the innocence of birth
Maybe we could save this land
And ease the pain with child-like hand

Two Eyes

Two eyes are still closed tightly
To the beauty of this earth
A face still glistens brightly
From the miracle of birth

Two eyes, a flickered movement
As a new life is unfurled
But the wonder of this moment
Is just wasted on this world

Two eyes begin to open
And in wonder gaze around
Youth's bud begins to ripen
As those eyes grow big and round

Two eyes born out of innocence
See the world with rosy hue
Still blind to all the violence
And the evil that men do

Two eyes are filled with anger
As they open to the truth
The mirror holds a stranger
Something missing from their youth

Two eyes now disillusioned
And ashamed of their own kind
In a torment of confusion
Now they wish they were still blind

Two eyes have now grown cynical
Against this world of pain
They've reached and passed life's pinnacle
And soon will close again

Two eyes are quickly dimming
And their light is fading fast
The world about is swimming
As they look into the past

Two eyes now close forever
At their owner's final breath
In that face like wrinkled leather
Lying peacefully in death

Runaway Train

Happy haddock, willow tree
Humpty dumpty, silver sea
Ping pong, bunny, apple pie
Singing haystack, purple sky
Little teapot, grinning cat
Talking horses, silly hat
Parcels, ribbons,tiny tots
Sky blue pink with polka dots
Roasted peanuts, candy floss
Silver moonlight, springy moss
Rainy Mondays, growing grass
Snakes in apples made of glass
Rocket, lolly, unicorn
Bugle, trumpet, rhino horn
Mary poppins, poppy seed
Bill and Ben and little weed
Wibble, wibble, blibble blime
Honey suckle, twist of lime
Silly sausage, carrot top
Pc Plod and Mrs. Mop
Ivor engine, rousing song
Hanging baskets, Babylon
Wizard, fairy, crimson grape
Icy snowflake, sticky tape
Milky, milky, gooey cake
Yellow roses, frying stake
Choking laughter, falling star
Deafened by a bridge too far

Floating sofa, fishing gnome
Smokey bacon running home
Howdy doody Mr. Spoon
Comfy ceiling, tiny room
Birdies tweeting, bouncing ball
River deep and building tall
Spotty toadstools, angel sings
Brainy badger, ravens wings
Giant beanstalk, puss-in-boots
Mother Goose in big black boots
Scented candles, ticking clock
Climb the ladder, on the block
Round in circles, chase your tail
Falling ashtray, sirens wail
Cabbage corner, smoking joint
Woven basket, needle point
Wedding bells for dusty bin
Bright confetti, creeping sin
Dancing oysters, pea green boat
Bright balloons, they bounce and float
Snowball fights in sylvan woods
Burning crosses, pointy hoods
Teeter-totter, swinging tyre
Metal monsters, spitting fire
Gaudy pennants, coloured plumes
Silent children, cloying fumes
Jingle, jingle, sleigh bell rings
Rising waters, acid stings

Test-tube babies, empty beds
Missing limbs and extra heads
Smiling faces, staring eyes
Crawling beetles, buzzing flies
Mellow music, padded white
Baggy trousers, jacket tight
Platitudes, a bright new pin
Oblivion is closing in...

Mice or Men?

You may call this life a rat race
But to me the only rats
Are the ones in spangled uniforms
Or suits and bowler hats

The rest of us are only mice
All chained to life's tread-mill
While the rats ride on the gravy train
And eat and drink their fill

They are living in the manner
They have grown accustomed to
While the masses pay in blood and sweat
For the lifestyle of the few

They enjoy all of life's comforts
Never wanting for their needs
While the masses live in penury
Victims of their leader's greed

To them our fate is just a game
As they play dice with our souls
The masses are expendable
To their power crazy goals

And when the final war arrives
They will be the first to hide
In concrete bunkers down below
While the masses burn outside

Don't you think it's time to show them
Whether we are mice or men?
We should put the rats back in their cage
And then try to start again

One Question, Lord

Lord, I know I've never prayed
And I really don't know how
But I feel there is a question
That I have to ask you now

The bible says you made this earth
From the void in just six days
Then displayed your love of beauty
In a myriad different ways

You started off creating time
By dividing day from night
And set the eternal cycles
With the darkness and the light

On the next day of creation
Your great wisdom you did show
Dividing vapours up above
From the waters down below

On the third day you continued
Separating land and sea
And set the plants to grow there-in
In a vast abundancy

On the fourth day you decided
On a focus for the light
You made the sun to watch the day
And the moon to rule the night

On the fifth day you created
Fish to swim the lakes and seas
And birds to fly upon the wind
And nest within the trees

On the last day you excelled yourself
Making beasts to roam the land
Be they crawling on their bellies
Or upon their legs to stand

Now, I know you will not like this
But there's something I must say
I think you made a big mistake
On that sixth and final day

It's a shame you were not happy
With the beauty of this land
For you blew it all completely
When you formed from clay a man

On that day you made a monster
Filled with anger, greed and hate
And he set about destroying
All the work you'd done to date

He is killing off your creatures
At a truly frightening speed
And the only reason for it
Is his never ending greed

He pollutes your seas and rivers
And he doesn't seem to care
That the life-style he is living
Is now poisoning the air

In his task he is relentless
Destroying all things in his way
He can now reverse your process
Of creation in a day

If things carry on much longer
It won't matter anymore
That the world is slowly dying
He'll destroy it in a war

So Lord, I now beseech you
Will you listen to my cry?
I only have one question
And that question Lord is Why?

Faulty Goods

Dear manufacturer
Your product I've returned
There are one or two malfunctions
In its workings I have learned

I cannot find the on switch
For the thing you call a brain
I did try to jump start it
But it blew up with the strain

I did an inventory
And there is a missing part
It was there in the instructions
But I couldn't find the heart

And the thing you call a conscience
Are you sure that it was there?
However hard I looked for it
I couldn't find it any-where

So therefore manufacturer
I'm returning your product
There's basic'ly just one thing wrong
It is completely f**ked!

Letter to Santa

Dear Father Christmas
I do not want lots of gifts
I am not writing to you
With my usual Christmas list

This year it is different
There's just one thing I would like
And it's not a new computer
Or the latest mountain bike

Please Santa can you help me
For I do not want a toy
Could you turn me into some-thing
Other than a little boy

Because every little boy
Grows up and then becomes a man
And it's men who cause the problems
That are ruining God's plan

It's men who kill the animals
And fight in all the wars
In all the bad news I have seen
It's men who are the cause

I haven't got a mummy
And I haven't got a dad
No-one here will miss me
So no-one will be sad

So Santa can you help me
Can you make my wish come true?
Could you turn me into an elf
Then take me home with you?

Letter to the P.M.

Dear mister prime minister
I am not very old
But I'm writing you this letter
Cos it's time that you were told

My daddy doesn't like you
And mummy doesn't too
Cos daddy lost his job last month
And he says it's 'cos of you

Now mummy's got to find a job
So she can buy us shoes
And daddy now plays cards all night
But all he does is lose

My mummy isn't happy
Cos my daddy couldn't stay
He borrowed some-one's money
And the police took him away

And now we haven't got a house
Cos the bank man took the key
So now we all live in one room
In a smelly B&B

Now I know why daddy hates you
And I hate you just the same
You didn't do your job right
That's why you're the one I blame

Growing Pains

Grass is growing
The wind is blowing
Rises the sap
But it won't fill the gap
Blooming spring
Is a transitory thing
New shoots sprouting
Before my eyes
Everything dies...

But what of me?
What part do I play
As my soul rots away?
I live and breath
Day to day
My life slips away
I die
Good-bye
Finito, I'm gone
But life carries on

What mark have I made?
What plans have I laid?
Who knows?
Who cares?
The squirrel just stares
He knows
As he paws at the earth
With his scrabbly feet

For something to eat
For what it's worth
He knows
And he's happy
Til a dog appears
He pricks up his ears
The moment has gone
The race is now on

But what of the children
We leave behind?
Weeping and grieving
At our untimely leaving
Surely they give
Us some reason to live
They`re beautiful, dutiful
Ha! Just you wait
Til they grow up
And spit in your face
Dad, get off my case!
What does it mean?
Is it obscene?
Who knows?
Time flows
Grass grows....

Paper Dreams

Two headed horses climb the walls
The panther stalks the bubbled balls
Dead flowers grow across my bed
Ten fingers crossed by hand that bled
Glass tigers gamble in the stream
The unicorn rides through a dream
Blue thunder clouds roll cross the sky
Beneath the watchful wizard`s eye
The bottled gold, unwanted stands
Untouched by mortal human hands
And silent standing all around
Toxic tubes rise from the ground
The light above will soon grow dim
The time will come to sink or swim
The dolphin smiled, the angel cried
Certificates for those who died
In crystal castles on the hill
They're blind to all the blood they spill
In pigeon holes, in shadowed rows
Where heroes hide between Death's toes
And china lemmings on the edge
Stand in line to take the pledge
The infant smiling on the dead
The Devil bearing words unsaid
And on the moon the sleeping clown
Dreams of stars and falling down
Picture formed in empty air
Fades above the empty chair

White coat drifting through the door
Floating two feet from the floor
A fleeting pain beneath the skull
And once again the world grows dull
The face behind the glass looks on
Until this paper dream is gone

The Veil

Beyond the veil deft figures prancing
Round the candle flame they're dancing
Shadows flit across the night
Silhouetted by the light
A tiny crack of light appears
Akin to sparkling diamond tears
A slender finger touches mine
I feel it reach into my mind
Enlightened by a fleeting touch
I throw away my mental crutch
My soaring empty heart made whole
I rush to greet my kindred souls
But startled to the ground I tumble
All about me visions crumble
Weeping prostrate on the floor
The veil of life is closed once more

Pulvis et Umbra Sumus

Numbness fills this earthly shell
As darkness fills my mind
My eyes are open wide and yet
These mortal orbs are blind
A distant rhythm, soft and slow
Its echoes gliding past
The future slowly fades into
Old memories that don't last
The fading but persistent beat
Not easily ignored
Attempts to bind pure thought inside
This shell that never soared
The echoes slowly fade away
Forgotten for a time
The silence settles like a shroud
As chains of thought unwind
A key turns in a hidden lock
A darkness shrouded door
Now opens bleeding golden light
The shadow starts to soar
Then suddenly that distant beat
The pile of dust it calls
A shadow beckoned back to pain
And walking dusty halls

The Gate

An open gate
No love, no hate
Just numbness in your soul
Don't look, don't speak
No truth, no leak
One mind set on its goal

That vice, like ice
Now ain't that nice
That we are all friends here
One look, one book
Is all it took
To make the beast appear

No life, no hope
The endless joke
Is this the only way?
No light, no faith
This soulless wraith
Is cast in shades of grey

Is it too late?
Don't close that gate
A coin tossed in the air
A spin, a fall
A silent call
But who is there to care?

The endless start
No bleeding heart
Will ever be the same
Without the night
There is no light
The pawns are free from blame

Stranger in the Night

Hello again
Remember when
You walked this way before?
You lost your way
I came that day
And showed you to the door

Long years have past
Since we met last
Beneath this very tree
It's in your eyes
I'm not surprised
You don't remember me

You couldn't think
The demon Drink
Was driving you insane
All hope had died
In grief you cried
"The Devil take this pain!"

You know me son
I'm never one
To let a chance slip by
You had that look
I grabbed my book
And bid my demons fly

I came to you
At once you knew
Your thoughts and mine were one
You signed your name
I'm free from blame
You knew what you had done

Your wife returned
And soon you learned
Your son was on his way
For seven years
No pain, no tears
The deal we made that day

Don't look alarmed
You won't be harmed
That's not my way at all
So play the game
You called my name
I just returned the call

Let's face it lad
You have been had
And now your soul is mine
The moral here
Is ringing clear
Be careful what you sign!

So now I'm back
From blue to black
It's time to take my hand
The deal was signed
So be resigned
You just ran out of sand

White Rabbit, Black Heart

I'm losing all sense and feeling
As I scramble through the cracks in the ceiling
When I make it to the top
I can feel my heart stop
And my mind and soul go reeling

I know that I am only dreaming
When I see that White Rabbit beaming
Then He takes me by the hand
Suddenly I understand
And my mind and soul start screaming

He tells me now that we are leaving
And it's easy if I start believing
We can see the dark threads
Flowing out of our heads
Let's go and see what they are weaving

Umbilicals of black are flowing
Like a cancer they are spreading and growing
Every time they touch the ground
I can hear a dark sound
And I feel the pain they're sowing

They burrow, the ground is bleeding
I can feel my humanity receding
With a stab of shame I know
As I watch the buds grow
All the pain our thoughts are seeding

The rabbit is softly crying
I can see that He is ailing and dying
With a sudden cry I see
He is crying for me
All the time my eyes were lying

I feel myself slowly sinking
As I realize I just began thinking
With a final mournful wave
One to last me to the grave
Up above the Rabbit is shrinking

The light of day comes back creeping
And I see that I was only sleeping
When I open up my eyes
I frown and realize
In the night I have been weeping

All From a Carton of Orange Juice (Part 2)

I am the self,
Intrinsically identical.
The self is the ego,
The self is the id;
But neither the id
Or the ego exist.
Authentic identity,
Equivalent unity,
Selfhood in personality
Substantial speciality
Bigwig influenced materiality
Is all an error of subjectivity.

The soul is in main part the essence
of interior music.

Insubstantial thing, spirit.
The essential part is the vigouress
Temperament of life, fuelled by the
Meaning of vigor and the restless
Affectations of moral sensibility.
Have courage, ghost!

I, myself, am number one,
My real self, inner self, inside and out.
My inner being is an outward person,
A character, a credential letter,
Acting in humorous repute of the
Modality of nonconformist number and form.
I am, by virtue, an individual
Unrelated to the non uniform original.
One special being, existing in existence.
A person, an object, a unit of substance
Woven from the vague meanderings
Of an insane mind, made in the image
Of a long dead God.
I am that God, that God is me
I think therefore I cannot be.

Alphabetical Listing

Also by Phil Gibson

ISBN 978-1-4478-0570-0

A collection of Dark Poetry exploring the shadow side of human nature. If you have ever looked at the world around you and thought there was some-thing terribly wrong then you may connect with these poems. Written by one who is still an optimist despite knowing some-thing awful is going to happen!

Available from Lulu.com:

http://www.lulu.com/product/paperback/apocal
yptic-visions/16437858

ISBN: 978-1-4478-0620-2

This collection offers a peek beyond the mask of the author. The glimpse is brief and partial; sometimes sad, sometimes funny, sometimes serious, sometimes whimsical but always candid. Look into my eye, it's time to see what hides down that rabbit hole...

Available from Lulu.com:

http://www.lulu.com/product/paperback/beyond-the-mask/16427554

Connect online

Twitter:

http://twitter.com/#!/PhilG_Poetry

Facebook author page:

http://www.facebook.com/pages/Phil-Gibson-Poetry

Facebook book pages:

Apocalyptic Visions - http://www.facebook.com/ApocalypticVisions

Beyond the Mask - http://www.facebook.com/Beyond.the.Mask

Apocalypse and Beyond... -

http://www.facebook.com/pages/Apocalypse-and-Beyond/284526894939267

Smashwords:

https://www.smashwords.com/profile/view/phil gibson

Lulu paperbacks:

http://www.lulu.com/spotlight/PhilGibson

Phil Gibson Poetry:

http://philgibsonpoetry.co.uk/

Phil's blog:

http://philgibsonpoetrythegarret.blogspot.com/

www.ingramcontent.com/pod-product-compliance
Ingram Content Group UK Ltd.
Pitfield, Milton Keynes, MK11 3LW, UK
UKHW020222250726
13967UKWH00001B/138

9 781291 226911